Russian Bride
A Quick and Dirty Guide to Meeting, Dating and Marrying A Russian Woman

By Ivan Asimov

Table of Contents

Chapter 1. Introduction

This guide will walk you through, step by step, meeting the perfect Russian woman by giving you all of the information you require about the Russian culture as a whole and about Russian women in particular. It will train you in the art of engaging in natural yet invigorating conversation with her whether you meet online or in person. It will teach you how you can easily spot scams and other websites that prey on single men searching for their Russian soul mates, as well as informing you as to how you can pick out the right online dating site that will suit your needs. You will learn how to communicate with Russian women via email with confidence as well as spot potential scams and problems early. We'll analyze all information you need to know about your first trip to Russia to meet a Russian woman, including the cultural differences you must be aware of when meeting her and her parents. It will educate and prepare you for the monotonous and potentially expensive task of getting your future wife legal access to your country, if you plan to be married at home instead of her country, and have your marriage accepted by your country's laws and precedents pertaining to marital statuses. And finally, it will talk about the process of adapting and assimilating your new beautiful Russian bride, into the jumbled up ways, of this new age American lifestyle that we have created.

You cannot draw boundary lines on your heart. However, the boundless region inside of you that makes it possible to feel such a strong attraction to someone, does not grant you free access to all of the man made boundaries of the world. Falling madly in love with someone in a different and foreign part of the world is the most romantic love story you could possibly have for how you and your wife met. Unfortunately, there are some legal guidelines and restrictions that stand in the way of marrying your foreign lover, and bringing her back to your home country.

Throughout the pages of time, men have always been known to fall for the exotic women of Russia because of their beautiful accents, extraordinarily gorgeous features, and simply because they are mysterious women from a faraway land; they're not the cookie-cutter women at home, formed by the requirements and expectations of American society.

Another major attractive feature of these Russian women is that they were raised with very strong family morals, and with the absence of copious amounts of money clouding their life perspective on the true values of family, they make much better wives, and are less inclined to leave you during times of financial turmoil. It has been proven statistically, that married couples containing at least one partner that has lived in a period of financial depravity or poverty have a lower risk for divorce if money should unfortunately become tight. Would you not love to have a caring and compassionate wife, who values your children and yourself over her designer handbag, and a massive accumulation of shoes? Without being accustomed to all of the frilly fringe benefits of being an American woman, Russian women are easier to fall into and sustain love with, because they have been raised in a simpler lifestyle.

Unfortunately for Russians but fortunately for single American men, due to reconstruction of this post-communist country and the financial problems inherent within, Russian women have begun to look for husbands outside the boundaries of their home lands, searching for men who can take care of them emotionally as well as financially. This is where the phrase "mail order bride" has been derived from. Though these Russian beauties seeking American men generally have a stigma attached to them when other Americans hear about it, they don't view it as selling themselves into some derivative of slavery, but instead as a chance for a better life, in a land free from all of oppression and poverty still present throughout Russia.

An unfortunate downside to falling in love with a beautiful woman outside of your citizenship's national borders is the immigration and assimilation process associated with bringing a new citizen into your country. While it may be physically easy to move your new bride into the United States, the immigration laws governing the land take a gratuitous amount of time to process and recognize her legal living status. The shortest time it could possibly take to process her visa application is two weeks, and it generally takes between two weeks and a year to fully process. Apart from simply the time spent on paperwork and processing time, you also have the costs associated with filling out the paperwork, which generally cost a minimum of two hundred American dollars, and can reach upwards of seven hundred dollars!

Of course, you cannot put a price on love and true happiness. It is said that the greatest things in life are free, but that is only applicable if you are not willing to invest your time and money into something amazing. Apart from the costs of moving your bride back to your homeland, and the costs of the paperwork, you also have the costs of travel expenses you may incur when you travel to Russia to visit her for the first time before you fall hopelessly in love. While it is true that it may cost a lot to travel overseas and stay in the country for a few days, it is a risk millions are willing to take, to find their soul mate and eternal happiness. Be prepared however, to experience a drastic change in cultural climates as you leave the United States and enter Western Europe, because the wealth distribution in North America has made many citizens accustomed to a higher standard of living that is not considered standard in many parts of Russia, small towns in particular. This is partially why many of these beautiful women seek to escape the country and move to America to live happily and freely with a handsome American man, who can easily provide for the entire family you will have together.

All of this time and money spent can be very difficult, and it usually ruins any plans you had to run off for a romantic weekend and get married in the heat of a passionate moment, but waiting for your resplendent new Russian wife is definitely worth it. Once you get her visa and your marriage legalized, you must begin to work with her, on assimilating into American culture, as the cultural standards in Russia differ greatly. It is very important that you ease her into this process slowly, so she feels comfortable and accepted. Being a stranger in a new land can be stressful, hard on your spirit, and downright scary at times, so you will need to be well informed to help her along every step of the way.

Chapter 2. Everything You Wanted to Know about Russian Women

Russian women are often made out to be mysterious, enigmatic and different. This runs from presentation in many books to the same thing on numerous websites that try to inform you about Russian women and normally sell something to go with the advice as well.

But who are all these Russian women and why do they want to go to the West? Can't they find a mate in Russia? Why do so many of them become what are often referred to as Russian mail order brides?

Well, to answer the last question is, most of them had never probably heard the term mail order bride and don't think of themselves as such. In Russia there is no stigma attached to the term and the term actually doesn't exist on its own. Most Russian women don't view it as necessarily selling a Russian soul for American dollars; instead, they look at it like this: I am an attractive young woman and I have trouble attracting someone I like. I want it to be someone reliable. And the idea of travel appeals to me (as most Russians love to travel). So I will try to look around and see if I can fall in love with someone from a different country.

And yes, generalizing is never a good idea but the point is, contrary to skepticism of some people, you don't just "order" someone on the Internet and then some woman just shows up one day. Many Russian women are actually pretty picky about who they pick since they have more options than it may seem. The really good looking Russian women in particular.

But, still, why is it that there are no French mail order brides? British mail order brides? German mail order brides?

Well, the answer to that rests on the following factors: economic, social and physical/cultural.

First of all, let's face it; there is more economic opportunity in the West than in Russia, especially if you're from a small town and in a disadvantaged situation. This is not the case with Germany or Britain.

Secondly, Russian women greatly outnumber Russian men so local competition is harsh. Also, Russian men tend to drink a little too much and cheat a little too much. On the other hand, Western men can appreciate a Russian woman a little more as shown through higher standards of fidelity.

Lastly, physically Russian women are stunning. It's hard to generalize like that but in general, most Western men travelling to Russian will notice the abundance of good looking women. Furthermore, the cultural upbringing of many of these women makes them more inclined for a traditional lifestyle.

Hence the reasons why many Russian women want to find a Western husband. On the other hand, it is no mystery as to why a Western man would look for someone thousands of miles away: Russian women are hot and have many cultural traits that are perfect for building a traditional family. Thus, under the right conditions, a union can be a mutually beneficial arrangement for both the Western man and the Russian woman and even, dare we say, love and marriage.

Many American men feel that the pernicious influence of feminism of the 1970's has resulted in American women becoming more selfish and focusing on themselves alone instead of the family unit. As a result of this, the US society is being eroded, traditional values are dissolving, and sacrifice and commitment is replaced by selfishness, frivolousness and divorce. This shift in the structure of relationships has created a demand for something that is becoming a rare breed in America these days and it is a niche a Russian woman can fill.

As mentioned before the unique economic and social conditions of which prevail in both Russia and the West make the union of a Russian woman and a Western man start to sound like a perfect arrangement. It's interesting that I hear about women from Switzerland to the US bitter and hateful of all these Russian brides that come over. The truth is, in many Western countries nowadays women have trouble attracting men while men opt for the Russian brides. This results in bitterness on the sides of those women. But selfishness or independence as they like to call it, simply does not sell, so they only have themselves to blame that their men now want Russian women. I've seen heard of too many stories of older Western men that were cheated, betrayed and used by their selfish Western wives. So, is it really a surprise that they want someone different this time? I think not.

Another myth is one of a "passive, submissive Russian wife". Let me type it in CAPS so the message is clear: THERE IS NO SUCH THING AS SUBMISSIVE RUSSIAN WOMAN! SHE DOESN'T EXIST! As anyone that has been to Russia will tell you, Russian women in general are very far from passive. Actually, they can be very headstrong and bossy if necessary. Any Russian woman could probably take on a dozen feminists any day. But it is not her assertiveness that accounts for her desire; it is her strong sense of commitment, sense of purpose and family values that present her apart from her Western counterparts.

So, how is the actual process initiated? The Internet is now the most popular medium for Western men to find agencies that will arrange contact and eventually marriage with Russian women. There is also an option of meeting somebody in Russia. However most people opt for the Internet course initially for better or worse. In many cases, the Western man and the Russian woman will meet several times, in Russia, before the woman comes to the United States to live with her future husband.

Chapter 3. Online or Off?

Western men in search of Russian brides have more choices than ever due to the popularity of the Internet. Whereas back in the day mail order catalogs had to be distributed and contact was sparse and expensive, nowadays it's easier to use the web to scroll through pictures, initiate contact, exchange emails and even talk on the phone (direct or through an interpreter). However, there are still men who prefer to meet the women in person for a variety of reasons.

So, many men ask me whether it's better to go to Russia and meet a Russian woman there or go through an agency. Just like everywhere, there are up and downsides to each option. Let's analyze both.

Using the Internet to find Russian brides is both a time and money saver. From the convenience of one's home, a man can browse through online profiles, pictures and descriptions of Russian women. The first advantage of that method as compared to travelling to Russia is obviously the low cost. Searching for profiles and reading descriptions is free for on most sites. Furthermore, using search filters you can sort through hundreds of profiles using specifically desired attributes such as body type, hair color, education and more.

Thus, if you are just dabbling with the idea of dating a Russian woman, that would be the first way to go: you can get an idea of what Russian women look like and "sound like" through their profiles. Obviously, if you have to go to Russia just to look around, the cost of the tickets, hotel and food will be very, very high. Now if you look around some sites get to a point where you actually are considering contacting a Russian woman, the costs of the subscription and the interpreter on Russian bride agency will drive your expenses up. However, expenses still won't be nearly as high as a trip to Russia. For just a cost of membership to a website that matches Western men with Russian women, you can have access to thousands of potential profiles and save some money.

However, that's not the whole story. There are also disadvantages of using the Internet to find a Russian wife. This is one of the prime reasons many men decide to meet someone in Russia as opposed to online. That reason is the abundance of online scams of all sorts. These scams change from very basic to fairly elaborate but are united in the goal to scam you out of your hard earned money one way or the other. Going to Russia and looking for a woman there, while it does not guarantee freedom from scammers, still makes it a little less likely that those two eager girls you've been corresponding with are really part of an elaborate scam operation. Furthermore, not all of the women who sign up for such sites are serious about finding a Western groom. Many just want to try it and are curious; those need to be sorted out. In addition, some find it harder to connect with someone on an emotional level through emails and instant messages or even phone, without meeting in person.

Traveling to Russia to look for a Russian bride appeals to many men because of the level of personal connection that can only be made when meeting face-to-face. Furthermore, there is chemistry that can be felt in person that could not be experienced over the Internet, thus making the Internet more risky. I personally have known many men who have initially liked the women they were corresponding with by email and phone only to discover that something was missing after the trip to Russia. That is a lot of money wasted for nothing. Thus, meeting in person to begin with does have its advantages. Also, there is a lower chance of scams when meeting in person because you both know the woman is a real person and that she is dedicated enough to take the time to meet you.

The high cost of airfare and lodging is one of the drawbacks to looking for a Russian wife in person. Another disadvantage is the miscommunication and awkwardness the language barrier could cause so some money for the interpreter and similar accommodations would be required.

Thus, these are the drawbacks and advantages of both methods. But which one is right for you? We have included two case studies that will help you:

This will include stories of BJ and Sam. Both of them were disillusioned with Western women. Both believed that mail-order Russian brides through the online websites were definitely the quickest way to find a Russian bride. Both learned that it was not the most effective way to obtain a good bride or marriage.

The internet has proved successful for some people. The advantages of this method are that it creates a basis of communication and is convenient for those who lead busy lifestyles or lack opportunities to meet new people. Not everyone has the time nor means to physically search for potential spouses. It is expensive to make numerous trips to Russia to meet a new woman without some focus or aim. However, using the internet can result in negative outcomes. The disadvantages are that honesty on both ends is always going to be questionable on the internet, and connecting through the web can be a lot different than actual confrontation. Given the best of communication styles, there is always the chemistry between two people that is difficult to project via the internet.

If you are keen on marrying into the Russian heritage, why not first take a trip to the country where your future bride would come from? Russia is very fruitful in culture and history with tasteful cuisine and intriguing traditions. Its' main cities of Saint Petersburg and Moscow are home to plenty of tourist areas like Red Square, Kremlin, and Saint Basil's Cathedral, as well as the Bolshoi Theater.

The more you know, the more successful you will be in your endeavors. And like they say, the best way to learn a language is to travel to the country which speaks it. The best way to understand the culture and intentions of the women you'll meet is to see it first-hand, and the best way to learn that which books cannot teach is to experience it for yourself. Many single, goodhearted Russian women reside in the areas you'd choose to visit, and just as on the internet, many of them are extremely interested in English-speaking men and are waiting to be swept off their feet.

Chapter 4. Online: Picking the Right Agency

Like any other type of dating service, it can be difficult to find a bridal agency website that fits your needs. The Internet is full of offerings, just search for Russian brides and gazillions of websites come up. A lot of people are interested in Russian brides and naturally people want to cash in on the trend. Unfortunately, this attracts a lot of unscrupulous or even dishonest characters as well. Thus, as they say, buyers beware. However, the opposite extreme can also be a problem as there are many trustworthy sites out there and plenty of Russian women looking to find a mate, not just scammers looking to make a quick buck over you. It's a nice problem to have, but it can confuse you and make the selection process more difficult.

Selecting an agency that is reputable and fits your requirements is one of the determinants of how successful and cost efficient your voyage will be. If you're serious about starting and maintaining a relationship with a Russian woman, the process can easily get frustrating if you aren't careful about which types of agencies you join.

Why even care whether you're dealing with a large agency? What difference does it make as long as you can find the woman you need? Well, there are several considerations to take into account when making this decision. First of all, you want an agency that has some kind of strong anti scam policy and a verification system to make sure that each participant on the female side at least seems serious about this. Browse the agency's website and check to see if there is any kind of a screening and verification process that women have to go through before they are listed on the website.

If there isn't, you might want to click on that Back button and try somewhere else.

"But why?" "Look at all those hot women on here, who cares if they were screened or not?" Well, it is very tempting after looking at all those profiles to join and write to a girl or even several. But if they were not screened and the website themselves is unaware of who is actually registering on the female side, who's to say if that girl is really the girl in the picture? Or who's to say that the person posting that picture is a girl at all? Due to high proliferation of scams in this industry, signing up for any such website may be a waste of money at best and compromising your credit card information at worst. And it doesn't even have to originate in Russia, plenty of American scammers had been creating sites with thousands of fake profiles with enticing photographs to get men to provide their card info and never hear from anyone ever again.

Thus, if the agency states that they don't verify the identity of the women or if the agency doesn't state anything on the topic, steer clear of them. Another sure sign is extremely short or cookie cutter profiles demonstrating no real personality or interest on the part of the imposter.

For example: "sexy!" or "looking for reliable man 32-50". Yes, these are actual examples. Now, what's wrong with that picture? Well, first of all here is (presumably) a woman (and very good looking one at that) that wants to meet her life partner, the man of her life and to represent herself the only thing she can put into a profile is "sexy" or "looking for reliable man"? I mean, either this woman is not of the brightest bunch or it's not really her. You can never know for sure but I'd be willing to bet $15.99 that someone created that profile and put it up together with a bunch of others just to present this look of thousands and thousands of profiles. If someone wants to generate thousands of profiles the easiest thing to do is write these short and cryptic descriptions. So, this is a definite red flag if you don't want to waste your money. Of course, if the profile is more extensive it could still be fake. However, it would take too much time to put up thousands of those profiles by the website owner. Thus, if descriptions seem more elaborate (a few paragraphs at least) and there is a difference between each profile, the agency is probably not putting those things up by themselves.

When browsing around a prospective agency's website, it's important to pay attention to what you're viewing. A skillfully designed website with a professional appearance isn't always legitimate, but it's a good clue as to what kind of business you'll be dealing with. As you view the profiles provided, ensure that each has an extensive amount of information with plenty of details and photos- not just a name, age, and head shot.

Once you've found an agency that looks authentic, you'll need to do some more legwork. Read any reviews you can find via an internet search and look for helpful commentaries from those who've already used the agency's services. You'll also need to follow up on agency contact information provided- email addresses, phone numbers, etc. Checking the scam agency database is also wise.

With just a bit of amateur sleuthing, you'll be well on your way to finding an agency that is the perfect fit for you. These tips should help you find a reputable agency that will assist you in finding the bride of your dreams.

Chapter 5. Scams: Spotting Problems Early

By doing a quick internet search, you can find plenty of websites where visibly, single Russian women are looking for other single, typically English-speaking husbands. But just as easily, you can find an abundance of websites which tell of scammers, or the said "dream" women who have cleared plenty of bank accounts as well as hearts.

A word to the wise: The quickest way to spot a scam is by searching match-making websites for authenticity. Websites for communication with Russian women should have approved seals by the Better Business Bureau and/or anti-scamming associations. You should also check to ensure that the label is genuine, and not fake. Explore the label in a little more detail. Check to see if there are references from satisfied customers. See if you can talk to satisfied customers. Also, non-scamming Russian based websites are slightly more difficult to come by than websites which are based in some other country. Take the opportunity to locate a service, if you have the opportunity to visit Russia as part of your research process.

Many new websites are not to be trusted unless they quickly build a good reputation. The very best websites are those which maintain notability to their name, have a history of operation, are mentioned in several places and maintain a level of popularity. Keep in mind, just because a website seems large and well-used may not mean it is a veritable source. Take the time upfront to do the research; it will pay off in the long run.

16

As far as scams from various women and scammers posing as women go, there are always new and evolving scams but it's a good idea to keep an eye out for the following things:

1. Unlikely stories about a mother or a relative ending up in the hospital and how $2000 is needed right away to save them. Likelihood of that being true is slim to none.
2. Stories about how the university tuition is going up and $500 is needed right away to help.
3. Pay for the apartment because she has no place to live (and she is sick of living with grandmother)

If people made a rule not to send money to anyone in the above two cases, most common scams would have been prevented. And, yes, I have heard several people (a large minority) who have sent money under premises similar to above and the woman not lying and the whole thing not being a scam. However, they are a very small minority. Thus, if you do decide to do it, be sure you are very, very confident about this woman and thus relationship. When in doubt ask somebody Russian as what you ascribe to cultural differences can sometimes be nothing but scams.

Another common scam involves you going to Russia and basically paying for food, entertainment, housing. After that the girl disappears. Along the way she will also try to milk you for as many gifts as she can. The only guarantee against that one is advice from someone else Russian who is on your side and your own good judgment. Look for serious women looking for serious relationships and the chance of that occurring will be minimized.

Chapter 6. Communicating Over Email

Be aware that some scamming sites employ Russian women to scam you through your personal e-mails with her, and these types of women are experienced in roping you in. Also know that just because the website is verified, it does not mean that the women you contact are not scamming you in other ways. The first and most obvious clue of this is if the woman is overly-enthused to have you visit them or to visit you. This brings in the discussion of money rather immediately and suggests the possibility of you paying for something that could end up being taken or transferred to them.

Another obvious clue is if the woman promises undying love and devotion on the first contact. Pay close attention to her emails – do they read like conversations or scripts? Does she say the same thing over and over again? A woman communicating to get to know you will ask you questions about your life, what you do and share the same about her personal life. If the woman does not seem to be interested by asking questions, responding to your own, this is not solely a language barrier and is likely bogus.

If the woman uses references to costs she cannot afford, like money to pay for learning English or the internet cafe to e-mail, this is another presumably very obvious sign. If money is transferred to her for any small reason, she will begin to realize that she can create other costs through various monetary excuses and sympathy. This should seem very obvious but there are many forms of manipulation used in hopes that you will fall victim to any deception.

You should also know that even after months of communication, genuineness is not guaranteed. There are many scam stories where the problems did not start for months, years, or ever until after marriage. That doesn't mean you need to be paranoid and distrustful of everything, but being naïve about the probability of that happening is just as unwise.

Pay attention to the way a woman communicates with you over initial few emails. What words does she use, how does she phrase things? Does it seem like she is a little too eager? Despite the translation, many cues can be picked up from people's conversations that can save you time and money down the line.

Chapter 7. Travelling There: Your First Trip

If you do end up meeting a Russian woman who does indeed seem to be right for you, and if you are ready to take the trip to meet her in person, you should indeed be very cordial and at your best upon first encounter.

As it may be, the best advice to take is to simply be you. Do take the time to spit shine every aspect of your being – hair cut, clothes, shoes, and fingernails. Your first impression will be lasting and the only chance you get for a first meet and greet – make it memorable. If you were romantic in e-mails, be romantic in person. Take her a small inexpensive token from the US (pick up something in the gift shop at the airport), to create good thoughts. Ensure that you don't frighten your potential bride. Be chatty and fun, but not over the top. Don't forget to smile. A few good phone conversations prior to the visit will tell you whether conversations will be interesting.

If you are a drinker, be sensitive to her issues. Alcoholism is a concern in Russia. If she has past history with alcoholism in her family, be sensitive to that and keep it in perspective at all times. Again, your objective is to let her meet you and to win her approval and love. Also, though drinking is more accepted and prevalent than in the US, tread lightly. You want to be careful, in the event it's a scam. You don't want to wake up with your wallet and passport missing in someplace you know nothing about.

Be cautious about falling into bed, engaging in sex, the first day. This can be especially dangerous if mixed with alcohol. Though Russian women can be more relaxed about pre-marital sex, you want to be sure that this is not another scam situation. Women use their bodies under the pretense of love to trap a man. Venture forth with eyes wide open; think with your correct head.

Make sure that you have activities planned during your stay. Your goal is to learn as much as possible about your future bride. This is accomplished more easily if you participate in joint activities while you're there. Russia is a beautiful country with a rich history. See the sights together. It's not about spending money or taking her shopping; it is about spending quality time together, talking, laughing and creating shared memories. Set your itinerary before you leave the US so that there will be no questions. Have her recommend her favorite thing to do and do that. Find out what sight she has not seen that she would like to see and share that new adventure together. See, taste and smell as much of her life as you can: It will help you make the right decision and aid you as you help her to transition to her new life in the US.

Be hopeful, but also understand that success is not guaranteed in any relationship. Going to Russia can be a very daunting experience to any person, let alone to greet someone they may be potentially marrying. Taking a chance is one thing, but any large leap shouldn't ever be taken too lightly, nor should it be misunderstood. Remember that not every date is successful, and chemistry over the internet does not necessarily mean chemistry in person. Read her body language. Don't get taken by the pretty face or nice body – be realistic. If she doesn't engage you, doesn't smile, doesn't converse about her life or shows interest in yours, then it's possible that she is not interested. Given this, if she doesn't terminate the meeting early, then it's probably a scam. If you find yourself sitting at the table and wondering why you came, then it's possible that it doesn't work for you as well.

As mentioned, be cautious. If you have arranged to stay with her, make sure that you have alternative arrangements. Don't give the impression that you are at all skeptical of the meeting, but do have a back-up plan or hotel in mind in case things do not seem to work to your benefit. Nevertheless, also remember to follow your instincts. These unions are necessary in finding the right one, and they should also leave you optimistic about your life with this person. Do not take it personal if it doesn't work. But again, if you take the time upfront to chat, email and talk prior to the trip, you will experience greater success.

Not every first trip will end in marriage. Be prepared to establish a good foundation from which the nurturing relationship can grow. As stated, you want to get to know her and she you. You want to create good first memories that you have something to talk about and share during future conversations and communications. You want to establish in her mind that you are the one and only, and leave her longing for more. Your second trip to Russia will be even more fulfilling.

Try to learn at least a little bit of Russian and buy a few books about Russian culture. Chances are her parents are old school Russians and will appreciate the cultural sensitivity as well as the effort to learn Russian on your part.

Chapter 8. Cultural Differences

During your trip, you should be careful to note the cultural differences in Russia. You do not want to accidently offend your potential bride. Following cultural norms will help the Russian woman feel more comfortable with the experience. Be aware that what you consider a courtesy may be considered an insult to someone with a different social background.

Try your best to respect the Russian culture during your visit. It is best to learn as much about the culture as possible before meeting the woman. If you do decide to pursue a relationship with her, you will need to be aware of the social norms to which she is accustomed. Be sure to openly communicate any confusion you may have about proper behavior. It's much better to ask a seemingly foolish question than to risk seriously offending her.

When first greeting your bride, be sure to be friendly and polite. A good first impression can help ease the initial meeting, but a bad one can make the situation awkward and uncomfortable. The Russian language tends to be very literal, so be careful about using phrases that may not intend a literal interpretation.

Marriage is a cultural norm in Russia. Typically, love is considered the only appropriate reason for marriage. If the bride does not show a desire to develop a romantic relationship with you, this may be a sign that she is trying to exploit you. Premarital sex is common, but cohabitation is not. Most Russians marry prior to age forty.

You should be aware of common superstitions in Russia, in case the woman's parents happen to believe in any. One common superstition is to never whistle inside the house (especially someone else's house) – brings bad luck. Another one is to not shake hands over a threshold (the entrance into the house), either you have to come in or they have to come up.

Be observant of the people around you. Try to take in the culture of the area and do your best to mimic others. Again, open communication with your potential bride can help you adapt more quickly. Consider reading books about Russia during your flight. The greater your understanding of the culture the smoother your experience will be.

Russians are very proud of their country, so do not say anything derogatory during your visit. National pride is very important aspect of Russian culture. Asking questions about the country in a friendly manner can help stimulate conversation. Russia has a rich historical background and there are many interesting things to learn about the country. Ask your potential bride for clarification about the history you've learned to show her that you're interest in her culture.

Drinking in Russia is a common social activity. Russians often drink more than what is considered acceptable in other countries. Do not be surprised if the woman drinks more than you expect. It is not a sign of alcoholism, but merely a difference in culturally accepted alcohol intake. It is not uncommon for a few people to drink an entire bottle of vodka during a social gathering. However, as always, use caution if it seems too over the top, especially if other unknown people are involved.

Chapter 9. Bridal Visas and Such

Just because love is blind, does not mean that it is also ignorant of all immigration laws. So, you have fallen in love with a beautiful Russian woman, and because of the immigration laws of Russia you are able to visit freely, even without a visa if you are an American citizen or a resident of any nation in the European Union. But what does this mean about your future together, and the process of bringing your bride to be, back into your native country? Well here is the cold truth, straight out of the bottle: unfortunately, bringing your bride back to the states to marry her, is not as easy as it is to visit her country. There are certainly a few snags involved with bringing a woman back to your country to marry, which are set in place mainly to protect the both of you from women seeking citizenship and not true love.

If you do not want to marry your bride in her native country, then there are several things you need to be informed of, before you decide to tie the knot. If you had any hopes of quickly fleeing Russia with your bride to be, and headed home to be wed, you had better be prepared to wait at least a couple weeks before your marriage and her entry into your homeland is legalized.

Whether you live in the United States, or a Western European country, there are very strict laws governing the visa eligibility for Russian women entering. Though the specific laws vary based upon your country of residence, the minimum waiting period before she is able to enter your homeland is at least two weeks, and it can sometimes take up to one year before she is legally granted access to the soil. This can be rather unfortunate if you were planning on a quick and romantic wedding, tying the knot in the heat of the moment. So it is best to apply for her visa as far in advance as you possibly can, as it could potentially take a great deal of time to be granted approval. In order to make sure that you are doing everything you can to expedite the process, be sure to communicate with the embassy of her country, and your country's customs division, as it may require some extra paper work on your part.

Apart from simply the time it takes to get a legal visa, it also takes a considerable amount of money to process and approve the visa. Of course, again, the cost much like the time required to process the visa varies by country. However, the average cost can be anywhere between $200.00 and $700.00 in United States dollars. Ouch! While it actually takes the longest amount of time to legalize her visa to enter the United States and become a legal citizen, the paperwork and legalization process is the most costly in the United Kingdom; neither of these countries make it very easy to follow the pulls of your heart when you decide the times is right to marry Russian beauty.

If you cannot afford to wait to be married or pay for the proper paper processing a legalized visa requires, it may be easiest and best for both of you to marry your bride in her native country. Whether you had planned on a beautiful, elegant wedding, or something that was a spur of the moment marriage during a romantic weekend getaway, you need to have patience and save up a considerable amount of money to ensure that the whole process transitions smoothly for her, as she will be moving and transitioning into a new land and you want her to be as comfortable as possible. The easiest way to move through this process is to maintain a calm and cool exterior, as fretting and becoming angry will only make this transition seem longer and become more uncomfortable for you and your bride.

Remember, that this transition is going to be potentially just as difficult, if not more, for her as it is for you. She will require your undivided attention and support as you both move forward in your journey towards your future together. Do not get discouraged by the first couple roadblocks that you might encounter with your new bride and the immigration process, just remember that she is also trusting you to provide for her, and she has made herself vulnerable as well, investing her entire life into your marriage.

Keep in mind that these days the US authorities are very weary of fake marriages involving Russian brides. Thus, be ready for numerous interviews and screenings from the day she arrives till years into your marriage.

Chapter 10. Welcoming Her into the US

As daunting as the experience was for you to travel to Russia and meet your future bride, it is even more so for her to leave family and home, travel thousands of miles to a foreign country to start a new life. To facilitate the transition, you want to do everything possible to make your new bride feel as comfortable and relaxed as possible. She is not just learning to live with you, but having to also learn a new language and customs not previously experienced. Making her feel welcome involves a series of activities that will make her acquainted with her new surroundings in a short period of time.

But like any great romance, it begins at the beginning. When picking her up from the airport, make sure that you park the car and greet her at an acceptable place, customs or baggage claim is preferable, depending upon security measures at the airport. It wouldn't hurt to have a printed sign with her name on it, so she won't have to hunt you down from memory or a three by five picture. Don't make the mistake of driving around the airport in hopes of finding her at curbside. You may lose your opportunity to make a great first impression in her new home. Carry her luggage and make sure it's all accounted for prior to leaving the airport. If you are romantic, continue the romance you began in Russia, have fresh seasonal flowers for her when she arrives.

Depending upon the time of day, plan a small excursion around the area prior to going home. Acquaint her with her new surroundings. Allow time for her to feel comfortable with the area and more importantly, to feel comfortable and relaxed with you. Take her for a light meal. Use this opportunity to discuss your future plans together – housing, marriage, work, travel, education, and children. These are probably topics discussed via email and during the meeting in Russia, but it's been a long flight and much time for second thoughts. Let her know you are serious about a life together with her in the US. Talk to her about how she will fit into your life, and about how she will be able to create a life for herself as your new partner in life. Now would be a good time to talk to her about the wedding and if possible set a date. You can also discuss obtaining her citizenship – classes she can attend, English language courses she can take. Don't go into much detail on these latter topics, just enough to let her know you want her to feel at home and a part of your life and society.

Welcoming her into the US includes making space for her in your life. Make sure that your home is clutter free, clean and that you have provided ample space for her things. Do more than just clear a path from the front door to the bedroom; make your home really shine. Vacuum, mop the floors, and clean the refrigerator and dust. Clean the bathroom and put the toilet seat down. Put fresh sheets on the bed and hang fluffy fresh towels in the bathroom. Clean the kitchen and purchase fresh food and vegetables. You should clear space in the drawers within which she can place her personal items. Hang empty hangers in the closet for her clothes. Make room for her in the bathroom cabinet. Make sure you have a vase for the fresh flowers. Make room for her in your life. If you have children, it might be a good idea to send them to spend time with the relatives for a couple of days. This will give the two of you time to continue the welcoming process.

If you haven't married, establish separate sleeping arrangements, at least for the first night or so. Remember, though pre-marital sex is accepted, it is not accepted to live outside of wedlock. If you only have one bedroom, be prepared to sleep on the couch. This may not be an issue, depending upon the nature of your relationship, but you certainly don't want to force it either. Give her time to relax and get to know you and her new home. Patience is a virtue that will provide you with many rewards.

If you can, take time from work to spend at least the first few days acquainting her with her new environment. Familiarize her with the local bus and/or rail service. Ride the public transportation system with her and take her shopping at the local store. Ask your friends and family to recommend a good hairdresser. Help her to become familiar with the local types of fruits and vegetables - they will be different than from her home country. Let her cook her favorite foods for you, and you return the favor. Acquaint her with as much of the American experience as you can afford. Explore such things as: taking her out to dinner, breakfast or brunch, to the movies, to the coffee house, the bookstore, for walks and dancing; plant a garden together to symbolize the beginning of your new life; let her see, smell and experience her new home. This is how she will learn to feel welcome and at home. This will also be the beginnings of creating cherished memories with you.

After a couple of days, introduce her to your family and friends. Plan a small dinner party or barbecue where she can meet and greet those close to you. Keep it simple and make sure that everyone has a part in the event. Try to have one of your relatives host the event, so that you can spend time with her, helping her navigate the situation. Personally introduce her to all your family and friends, don't just sit her in a corner and expect them or her to make the gesture. Have your favorite female relatives plan an outing for just the girls. If she is religious, take her to church and attend the service with her. Introduce her to your spiritual leader, if you have one.

Establishing the routine of life facilitates comfort. To be able to know and expect certain behaviors is nonthreatening. When you return to work, make sure that you leave her with a level of calm that you will return, what time she can expect you to return, and how she can deal with any situations that may occur in your absence. Make sure that she has an emergency call list. Allow opportunities for her to call home. She has certainly left family and friends and will feel more at home if she can on occasion reach out to them. Call her during the day, see how she feels, what she is doing. Teach her to use your universal remote control for the TV, and how to work your washing machine and dryer. Make sure she has money. If she has yet to understand the US currency, provide her with a debit card. Set aside a separate account so that she can learn our financial systems without interfering with the household account. Have your female family and friends check on her, and perhaps take her for an excursion during the day. If you've set the wedding day, use this time to plan the wedding.

Chapter 11. Adapting

Adapting to a new life takes time and patience. It involves making the changes required to live in the new environment. It is the process by which your new bride will come to exist perfectly in her new life with you. It is a state of being as much as a state of becoming.

The ability to adapt means that your new bride has the ability to live in her current new life. Change can have an effect on a person such that they become despondent, lonely for the people and places of their past. Extreme loneliness can, if left unchecked, bring about a state of depression. Depression can leave your new bride lethargic and lifeless. To combat this, you need to understand that she will require connection or tie to her old life. You need to communicate with her constantly to understand her needs and desires. Obviously making trips home can be cost prohibitive, but there are other things you can to do to combat loneliness.

As mentioned in the previous section, allowing occasional calls home is good for the soul. But even more than the occasional call, would be fellowship with people from her home country. Look for Russian communities and circles that she can acquaint herself with. Encourage her to make friends and escort her to outings in this new circle. I recommend escort because you don't want to expose her to elements that may have a negative effect on her mental state and persuade her to do something against the plans you and she have created together.

As you help her through this process, it is equally important that you help her establish new friends, American friends that can assist with the transition. Encourage her to make friends at your local church or community center. Encourage her to use her skills – sewing, singing, cooking, writing, decorating, planning, and hospitality – whatever it is in this new circle of friends. If she has no skill (which is hard to believe), assist her in identifying new ones. You want to encourage utility and a sense of belonging.

The ability to adapt is also measured in the ability to procreate – have babies. What better way to be useful and learn to adapt than to have children. If you haven't already, begin the dialogue. Acquaint her with all the support systems available to ensure a healthy outcome. Have her visit with your female family and friends of childbearing age. A healthy birth outcome requires as much a healthy mental state as it does a healthy physical state.

As you support her through this adaptive state of being by ensuring mentally stability, you need to also ensure that she continues to adapt to her new US home. This will require that you encourage attendance at English language classes and the pursuit of her citizenship. Assist her with the class registration, course materials such as books and supplies. Make sure that she knows how to get to and from classes. Help her with the studies, if she asks.

Another step towards adaptation would be to obtain a driver's license. If you live in a metro area that does not have ample public transportation, and you have an additional car, consider this option. Having a driver's license is a rite of passage in the US, and will provide her with the ability to handle her business during the day. She can do her shopping, attend her classes and even run simple errands for you – dry cleaners, banking etc. Make her feel a part of life, not like some doll on a shelf.

She may ask to get a job and make her own money. Though this can be perceived as a major step towards adapting to the new environment, it may signal discomfort to you. If your perception of having a Russian bride was to have mate that would never threaten you by making money or certainly not more money than you, this needs to be addressed prior to the marriage offer.

However, it is natural for a healthy person to desire to provide some sustenance. In third world countries, women tend the farm and animals. In the US, women get a job and earn money. As she adapts to her surroundings she will notice that other women work for a living, and may eventually come to desire the same. She will see this behavior emulated on television, in movies and around your community. You need to discuss this and come to a healthy decision that works for your family.

If you make enough money to care for the home and the basic needs, perhaps the discussion should be about allowing her to make play money, money for vacations, extra money for Christmas gifts, savings to buy a new home, build the baby nursery or savings for another car. It is understandable that you might not want her work after she has children, but what will she do prior to that? Her desire to work should be viewed as a way for her to assist in building your new life together, not as a way to demean your ability to provide. Open a joint savings in which you both share in building that future life together.

Chapter 12. Conclusion

Humans are by nature social beings. It is expected for a man to want and desire the love of a woman, and vice versa. The coming together of East and West is the perfect storm. Russian woman outnumber Russian men; the economic situation in Russia is unstable; Russian Men have attendance towards infidelity; Russian men tend to drink more. In the West, US men have come to believe that US women are over demanding and destructive of fundamental family values. The migration of East and West is just another branch in the evolutionary arm where humans venture out to ensure the survival of the race.

This is not to say that Russian women will give in to any whelm you have. They are, after all, human beings and endowed with all the idiosyncrasies of humans-the ability to discern good from bad, love from hate, joy from anger. You should approach this venture with a full understanding of what you desire in a mate and communicate those desires to your potential bride. Do not be lulled into thinking you are buying a slave. She is a sentient being.

Selecting the right bride begins with choosing the correct agency to mitigate your plans. Taking the time up front to choose the correct agency and understand the potential threats to you, will in the long run save you much heartache and misery. Do your homework. Ask questions, talk to others that have used the service with success. Learn the key indicators to look for. There are people out there that will scam you, take advantage of you. But there are also Russian women looking for genuine love, protection, and provision. You goal is to discern truth from fiction. Take your time and ask the right questions. Choosing the right agency will help you navigate this process.

Communicating your desires upfront and continually throughout the "dating" process is essential. Especially since this will occur thousands of miles apart. You need to talk or chat and do it often. Listen to what is being said and hear what she is looking for. The goal s twofold: Understand your future bride and eliminate as many surprises as possible. You will never learn everything, but you can come to understand the basics about this person. Do not be afraid to change your mind and make another selection. It's easier to do in the early stages versus after she has come to the country as your fiancé.

Make sure that you meet face to face prior to confirming the marriage deal. Physical chemistry should not be taken lightly, and can truly impede the ability to create the perfect union. If either of you finds no common attraction upon the initial meeting, you may find it hard to adapt to you new life together, and place your relationship in jeopardy. The inability to touch and be touched, to look someone in the eye, will create opportunities for either or both of you to seek that attraction elsewhere.

Though she may look like you and dress like you, there will be cultural differences. Take the time to learn the differences. Cultural differences expand beyond food and language. It also includes religion, a way of seeing the world, engaging other humans and completing the daily functions of life. The ability to welcome her and make her feel at home will be based upon your sensitivity to her culture. Though you desire to have her become a part of your world, forcing her to forego all that she is will result in neurosis and not lead to a healthy adaptation. Try, initially, for a blending of the two cultures.

Check with the US immigration office and have the correct Visas. No deal is done until the paperwork is finished. Don't make assumptions with regards to these matters. However, if you lack the resources to make this happen in a timely manner, or she prefers to marry in her home country, be prepared to assist her in the marriage – whether time or money. It's not that you have to pay for everything, but it will take additional resources for you to stay and get married. Nothing is more frustrating to both of you than to traverse down the road towards marital bliss only to determine that your paperwork is incomplete or wrong or missing. Handle your business.

Be ever vigilant about scams: It is prevalent on the Internet. Though your intentions are honorable, others may not share your sentiment, and will capitalize on your perceived weakness. Do your research upfront and select the right agency or service. Spend as much time talking, emailing, and chatting with your match. Listen for variety in her conversation, ask questions and, expect and encourage questions about your life. Ask for additional pictures of her and her family and friends. Be prepared to share additional pictures of yourself. Allow yourself ample time and resources when you do visit, to get to know as much about the match as possible before you ask for her hand in marriage. Have an agenda for your visit: Don't just go wondering aimlessly into Russia.

Once married, be flexible and patient at all times. Now that she has arrived, the real work begins. Making her feel welcome, assisting with the adaptation process will stretch the imagination of the two of you. She has come to your home, your country to make a new life with you, to make a home together. Honor her decision by helping her with the transition. If you've done your homework, know her culture, if you've communicated with her and met her prior to the Bride decisions and the trip to the US, it will be easy for you.

Don't forget to breathe, have fun and enjoy the experience of new love!